# NAUTICAL NO-NO'S

*"Nautical No-No's" is a collection of anecdotes chronicling the development of a sailor. It suggests what NOT to do, and what to do when you have done it!*

*From novice to sailor in seventy-nine easy lessons . . .*

## BY
## ELYSE AND ROBERT KATZ

## ILLUSTRATIONS BY
## CAROLINE YOUNG RHEAULT

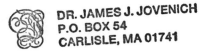

# Nautical No-No's

Copyright © 1980 by
## Elyse and Robert Katz

*drawings by Caroline Young Rheault*
*cover design by Jean Carvill*

Published by:
Shayna Limited
100 Andrew Street
Newton, Massachusetts 02161
617/244-1870

Library of Congress Catalog Card Number 80-50537
ISBN 0-9604208-0-0

# ACKNOWLEDGEMENTS

The authors wish to thank the people who helped make this book possible:

Caroline Young Rheault, the artist, whose drawings give a graphic dimension to our vignettes, has been a pleasure to work with;

A big thank you to our children, Sharyn and Andrew Katzen, and our number one crew, Gloria and Dick Miranda who have offered moral support, encouragement and editorial assistance during all the years of sailing and writing;

To our son David, our gratitude for providing the original inspiration that started us sailing;

Our grateful appreciation to Cecilia Fitzgerald, Celia Fitzgerald and Frank Horton whose editorial and technical assistance have been so invaluable;

To Jean Carvill, our thanks for the cover design;

A thank you to Herbert Gliick, editor/publisher of "New England Offshore", who suggested the format for this book, and to Barbara Shadovitz who helped with the preliminary editing;

And last, but not least, a thank you to our Sailboat Fairy for her inestimable help during our traumatic adventures.

We hope that the publication of our boating experiences will help others to avoid some of our problems and learn to cope with emergencies that always seem to occur. In other words: what NOT to do, and what to do when you have done it!

**Elyse and Bob Katz**

# CONTENTS

## THE ADVANCED SENIOR SEAFARERS

## ALMOST SAILORS

## THE SAILORS!!!!

# Prologue

It was 4:45 on a Sunday afternoon as Shayna sailed a close reach towards Mattapoisett Harbor. Flying a 130 genoa and full main she was knifing neatly through the famous, or infamous, Buzzard's Bay chop.

Suddenly a sharp report shattered the quiet. It sounded like a rifle shot from high overhead. Expecting to be dismasted, we were relieved to see the standing rigging intact. As the genoa came tumbling into the water it was immediately apparent that a halyard had snapped.

We luffed up into the wind to catch our breath, collect the sail and survey the damage. The downed genoa was easily recovered, the broken halyard removed and a No. 2 jib run up on another halyard. Within the hour we were on our mooring and reflecting on the few moments of excitement that had intruded upon a day of almost perfect sailing.

We had committed a "no-no". Earlier in the season when we repaired a worn section of the halyard we had failed to determine the cause of the excessive wear. Additionally, we had compounded the error by neglecting to check the halyard during the ensuing weeks.

This was hardly our first "no-no" nor was it destined to be our last. How did it all begin? Let us step back in time and chronicle the trials and tribulations we encountered along our course from novice to sailor.

# 1

# In the
# beginning . . .

No bells rang, no thunder clapped to indicate that this day would significantly alter the pattern of our lives. As we stood by the camp lake watching our son David maneuver a small sailboard we were struck simultaneously with the idea of sailing as a family activity.

Our brain storm led us to a course of action and we were soon enrolled in a basic sailing class given by the United States Coast Guard Auxiliary. Our commitment and enthusiasm made up for the fact that we had never even been on a sailboat.

We demonstrated true dedication by our tenacity in finding a place to park our car each week in crowded, college Cambridge. Only the hardy and determined passed that first obstacle to learning.

Thirteen weeks later we held two signed certificates attesting to our theoretical knowledge of sailing skills. Academically, we understood the principles of wind, water and boat.

Accompanied by our instructor, we were rewarded for our scholastic achievement by a short sail on the Charles River.

# 2           Whetting the appetite . . .

It was a cloudy, blustery March day, not really ideal for a pair of beginners. The choppy river, gusty winds and leaden sky were intimidating as we gathered our courage and bravely stepped aboard the nineteen foot Victory.

With our capable instructor at the helm, we reached, we tacked and we beat. Our classroom instruction had not detailed the heeling process clearly and visions of an unplanned swim in the Charles River plagued the distaff member of the family. Amazed to discover the angle of heel at which we did not capsize, I clutched the gunwales to keep from falling overboard.

Suddenly, another worry intruded upon my consciousness. The beastly weather had not deterred scores of other boats from zooming about the river, and we seemed to be on the verge of a collision course at all times.

When I realized that we would probably not capsize, and that near collisions were a form of sport, I began to enjoy the experience. There was no doubt about it: it was exciting, stimulating, thrilling. The realization was as great as the expectation.

As the Captain called, "Hard alee!" Bob and I dutifully ducked our heads and tended the jib sheets. We began to understand the boat's responses and enjoy the challenge it provided.

It was time to consider step two: the purchase of a small daysailer.

# 3 Search and ye shall find . . .

Each Sunday we pounced on the boating section of the newspapers to look for an appropriate boat for beginners. We wanted a boat that would be within our budget, yet accommodate four adults in reasonable comfort, and be forgiving of error by a novice at the helm.

Several promising prospects failed to satisfy our needs. It was late in June when at last we saw a sixteen foot fiberglass daysailer complete with sails, life jackets, lines and a trailer. She was sloop-rigged, had a pale green hull and proudly pointed her twenty-two foot mast to the sky as she set gracefully on the trailer.

Our prerequisites were satisfied. Her cockpit was roomy enough for four; all the equipment was included; it was a good trailer; the price was right. It was love at first sight and we bought her!

The seller gave us a lesson on how to rig the boat. He demonstrated raising the mast after first clearing the shrouds and spreaders from any obstacles. He repeated those instructions regarding the spreaders several times. At a later date we learned why.

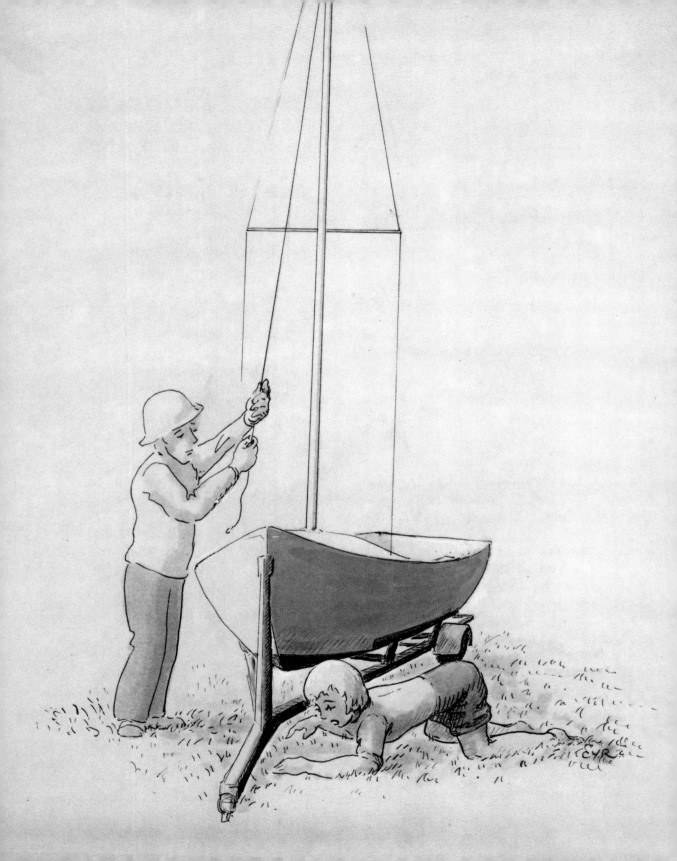

# 4

# One

# to get ready . . .

It was an impressive exhibition of the simplicity of rigging a boat. The seller easily raised the mast and was ready to lock it in place in a few fleeting moments. It looked very simple.

Now it was our turn. Nonchalantly, Bob clambered aboard, prepared to handle the mast, while I took a position at the bow. I was instructed to grasp the forestay by an attached line to help Bob balance the mast. When the mast was stepped, it was my job to secure the forestay to the deck fitting by an attachment called a clevis pin and lock it with a marine type safety pin.

With one hand I clutched the stay to center it in position, and with the other I fed the bolt through the fitting. Oh, for a third hand! To my chagrin, the locking pin squirted out of my hand into the grass. Needless to say, that was not the only time such an event took place.

Fortunately, on that day, and other times as well, that little piece of hardware was quickly located. The lesson continued as we learned to attach the boom and bend on the sails. Both mainsail and jib were easy to feed on their tracks and the whole sequence seemed a rather simple operation.

Despite our initial clumsiness, we soon mastered the art of rigging our boat in quick order.

# 5

# Two
# to get set . . .

Monday to Saturday seemed an eternity as we anticipated the thrill of the first sail in our very own boat! Our car was prepared for trailering by installing a hitch and electrical system. Finally, Saturday arrived and we went to pick up our boat.

The trailer with the daysailer was rolled down the driveway and easily attached to our car. Casually, the seller suggested that we not attempt to back the car without some practice. What an understatement!

We had no difficulty getting home, but parking the boat became a major project. In order to get the trailer off the street, we had to move it into the driveway. Back and forth we struggled in the confined area of the street. We visualized the ease that we had seen displayed by the drivers of tractor-trailers, but we couldn't duplicate their achievement.

When we backed the car, the boat-trailer swerved across the front lawn, careened straight for a tree, or jack-knifed against the car. Never did it go where we aimed it!

Finally, I got out of the car, stood in the street and tried to direct Bob to turn the car and trailer. That didn't work, so we reversed our roles. Back and forth I drove, to no avail, while Bob shouted instructions. In desperation, we finally disconnected the trailer from the car and Bob, making like a harness horse, pushed the boat-laden trailer up the driveway!

# 6

# And
# three to go . . .

As we trailed our daysailer along the highway to the state park, we were bursting with pride. It appeared to us that all eyes were turned our way with admiring glances for our little green boat.

Having no idea what to expect on the water, we had prudently left our watches, wallets and valuables safely at home. We packed a minimum of paraphernalia: life jackets, a thermos of iced tea, and various assorted expendable items.

The launching technique looked fairly simple when performed by the numerous power boats on the boat ramp. No one seemed to have any difficulty easing his trailer into the lake. Confidently, we proceeded to try to emulate the others.

Thirty minutes dragged by and we were still driving up and down the launch area shouting directions to one another while we tried to get the boat down to the water. Others managed this feat so easily whereas we drove up, down and sideways.

Finally we concluded that we would have to change our plan of action. It was decided to rely on brawn once again. I drove the car, manipulated its rear towards the lake, and then Bob pushed, pulled and lifted until the boat-trailer was lined up behind it.

The maneuver was effective but exhausting. However, we were finally in a position to back the trailer into the water.

# 7 **The first mishap . . .**

Almost too tired to continue, we stopped to catch our breaths before beginning the rigging procedure. After reviewing the rigging instructions we took our designated positions. Bob climbed aboard and readied the mast while I stood at the bow clutching the line attached to the head stay.

Bob levered the mast into its tabernacle, raising it, as I helped by pulling on the forestay. Suddenly, a sharp twang brought us to attention. Oh no . . . our first mistake! We had broken a spreader. Apparently, we hadn't loosened the shrouds sufficiently, and when the mast was pulled up, a tight shroud snapped off the spreader. Spreaders certainly seemed to be delicate objects!

So much for our first attempt to sail. There was no way to rig the boat with a broken spreader. We had no choice but to return home.

Dejected, disappointed and exhausted, we drove home. That we were still on speaking terms with one another proved the solidity of our marriage!

It was decided to use the rest of the day to learn to drive the car and trailer. We were determined and tenacious. We applied cold logic to the whole procedure and came up with a plan of action. Since Bob was the obvious one to push the boat off the trailer and winch it back on, it seemed reasonable that I should be the one to learn to handle the car and trailer.

After a couple of hours of unpressured practice, I learned to do a respectable job of backing up. Throughout the years, I perfected my trailering ability and basked in the admiring glances of others who had not yet acquired that capability.

# 8  But it's only a small dent . . .

On our next expedition we not only had a new spreader, but carried a spare since they seemed to be so fragile. Bob had been able to fashon these himself from aluminum tubing. Of course, we never broke another!

As we drove carefully along the highway, a traffic light suddenly turned yellow and Bob obediently stopped the car. The boat trailer, having no brakes of its own, kept on going into the back of the car!

Action and reaction. The laws of physics are such that once the trailer hit the car, it then bounced back. Fortunately, the safety chains attached from the trailer to the car, had kept the boat on a short leash and it hadn't strayed far. In the middle of the busy highway Bob had to brave the moving traffic to reconnect the trailer hitch. Another "no-no", of course: no sudden stops when driving with a trailer.

The dent in the rear of the car was hardly noticeable and represented our first battle scar! Our curiosity about the need for chains in addition to the ball-hitch was satisfied.

With no further incident we made it to the state park.

# 9       **Launched**
# **at last . . .**

Being ready to rig within ten minutes of our arrival at the launch area was a big improvement. We stepped the mast, attached boom and rudder, bent on the sails, launched the boat, parked the trailer and heaved a sigh of relief. So far, so good!

However, success was not to last. While I was parking the car, Bob was very busy bailing the cockpit. Was the boat leaking? No. We had merely neglected to insert the cockpit drain plug. There is another law of physics which states that water will seek its own level, and it was doing just that through the cockpit drain.

At last, we paddled away from the congested launch and mooring area, lowered the centerboard and timidly raised the sails. Uncertain about what would happen next, Bob grasped the tiller and held the mainsheet. I grasped the gunwales and held my breath!

Wonder of wonders—we began to sail.

# 10 **From hypothesis to conclusion . . .**

Theory is a handy thing to know, but practice and experience are necessary to make a sailor. Classroom instruction has to be applied to a practical application of its principles.

With the wind on our port side we were moving along nicely. The light winds and calm lake helped alleviate our nervousness. When the time came to change direction, Bob called out, "Ready about".

I prepared to handle the jib sheet and dutifully answered, "Ready". "Hard alee" came the next command. We ducked our heads and waited for the boom to come across. It didn't. Instead, the boat came to a dead stop, sails flapping uselessly. We were in irons.

Bob sculled the rudder until the sails were full once again. Gaining more forward speed before trying to make the turn, we repeated the tacking maneuver. We accomplished the come-about successfully and happily watched the main and jib swing to the other side as we headed off on our new tack.

We practiced our turns and began to feel more confident. We quickly learned that "tiller-towards-the-sail" is a handy reference to make a quick decision when preparing to tack.

# 11 **Another law authenticated . . .**

Enchanted by our first sail we headed back to the launching ramp. Rather than attempt to sail directly to shore amidst the numerous boats, we dropped the sails and paddled in. It would be a rare beginner who could sail to the launching ramp with ease.

I fetched the car and Bob easily nested the boat on the trailer. The mast was unstepped, the sails bagged, the rudder removed, the drain plugs opened.

When we tested the car and trailer lights, we discovered that we had done another "no-no". None of the trailer lights worked.

It was an inconvenient way to learn that it is necessary to disconnect the electrical system of the trailer from the electrical system of the car before the connections are backed into the water. Of course, everyone knows that water is an excellent conductor of electricity. Therefore, with car electrical system, trailer electrical system, and water, it was inevitable that something would short out. How fortunate that it was only two bulbs.

With neither signal nor brake lights on the trailer, we drove home cautiously. From that day on, we never failed to unplug the trailer's electrical system from the car. We also added waterproof lights to the trailer. In the five years we used that trailer, we never had another electrical problem, not even a burned out bulb.

# 12

# We can't climb on water . . .

One hot day on the lake we lowered the sails and dropped anchor so that the children, who had deigned to join us, and I, could dive in the water for a refreshing swim. Bob remained aboard to be sure the anchor held, since we weren't positive that a metal contraption dropped to the bottom of the lake would hold a boat in place. We had studied the theory of anchoring, but seeing is believing, and this was the first time.

Fully refreshed after our swim, it was time to climb back aboard. Bob lowered the line we had so carefully arranged for that purpose. It had a loop for the foot to step on, and a succession of knots arranged to enable us to grasp the line with our hands. Theoretically, it seemed more than adequate. In actual practice, it was a dismal failure! From a prone position in the water, there was no leverage to assume a vertical position as planned. Son David managed to leap aboard not unlike a flying fish, but daughter Sharyn and I struggled in vain.

We tried one foot in the loop and two feet in the loop. We lowered the line and raised the line. We grasped the gunwales and tried to hoist ourselves on board. We were pulled and yanked by the male members of the family. We got a foot on the boat, or a head, but never enough of the torso to make it all the way. It was obvious that we needed a swimming ladder.

Stranded in the water we had no alternative but to swim to shore. Since we had anchored fairly close to land, it was not a long swim. That was a fortunate state of affairs because our past exertions had exhausted us. When we reached the beach a friendly sailor gave us a lift on his sailboard. It was easy to step aboard the daysailer while standing on the sailboard.

No more trips into the water until we had purchased a proper swimming ladder!

31

# 13        Over the bounding main . . .

Boat launching by car was now done with great eclat! We could place the trailer anywhere we chose. We rigged with great competency and usually completed the entire cycle in about fifteen minutes.

The weekend weather continued to favor us each week until one lovely day the weather suddenly deteriorated. The wind began to gust and the lake acquired a chop—not terribly unusual for a hot summer day on the water.

For the first time the boat heeled more than we planned. The leeward rail was awash as we scrambled to put our weight on the high side in an attempt to lessen the angle of heel. We tried to spill wind from the mainsail, but the sheet had jammed in the cam cleat. The rigging setup of the daysailer included a spring held cleat hanging from the end of the boom. The mainsheet ran through that piece of hardware and was released by pulling the mainsheet away from the spring.

Unable to release the sail because of the pressure jamming the cam cleat, we became panicky and fought the tiller. We attempted to keep the boat upright by trying to ease the wind from the mainsail.

Our approach was wrong. Since we were unable to free the **mainsheet** and spill wind from the mainsail, we should have loosened the jib and released the tiller to allow the boat to head itself into the wind. When left alone, sailboats are designed to turn themselves and head into the wind without help from the crew.

# In the drink . . .

As we fought the wind by pushing against the tiller, we managed the ultimate "no-no". We capsized!

One minute we were staring at the horizon, and the next we were looking at the water below and the boat above. The boat was our cocoon and we swam out from under it. With our craft upside down, our personal belongings were either floating about or rapidly sinking to the bottom. It was too deep to retrieve the anchor and all the other goodies our self assurance had allowed us to bring on board. Our dignity and self esteem suffered immeasurably.

In addition to the trauma of being in the water, it was very difficult to right our centerboard sloop. The centerboard had slid back into its housing and was not available to provide the leverage as described by the "how-to" books. Fortunately, we were soon surrounded by several boaters eager to help.

Bob swam under the boat to release the main and jib halyards so the sails wouldn't act as sea anchors. Two men joined us in the water and provided the necessary strength and weight to get the mast pointed in the proper direction, towards the sky.

When we finally returned to the launching ramp to winch the boat onto the trailer, it seemed to weigh a ton! It probably did. In place of our lost belongings we had acquired hundreds of pounds of lake water between hull and liner. Some friendly sailors with strong backs, along with the winch, managed to get the vessel onto the trailer. The car labored to haul the heavy boat up the ramp so that we could pull the drain plugs. For an endless time water poured from her drain holes.

We learned another lesson the hard way! That was the last time we ever used a cam cleat on a small boat. We changed the mainsheet hardware so that it ran freely and was hand held. Many years later when we sailed our third boat for the first time and clutched the mainsheet in our hands, our broker, who was aboard for our maiden voyage, exclaimed, "I can tell you people have been small boat sailers!".

# 15                                   New
                                 horizons . . .

Lake Chaubunagungamaug, meaning "you fish on your side and I'll fish on mine, and nobody will fish in the middle," otherwise known as Lake Webster, seemed a good place to challenge our steadily improving sailing skills. On the Masschusetts-Connecticut border, an hour away, it offered a public launching ramp, parking for car and trailer, rest rooms, beach and bath house. It consists of several sections of lake connected by narrow channels and dotted with occasional islands.

The boat was launched without incident and we were soon under way. With the wind blowing a delightful eight to ten knots, we ran for several hours. We admired the scenery and memorized the location of some distinctive looking homes to guide us on our return. That lake is not a charted area.

We lost all track of time until we noticed the sun heading for the horizon. When we reversed direction to return, we discovered that we had made an error in judgement. Because we had been running with the wind behind us, we would have to beat into the wind on our return. It was soon obvious that it would be a long slow sail back to the launch ramp.

# 16    **Wind is free, but . . .**

Sails close to the wind makes for slow sailing. After sailing about two-thirds of the distance to the launch area, we found ourselves making no forward progress in a narrow channel. As a matter of fact, we seemed to be moving backwards!

The fact that some lakes can have strong currents was made known to us at that time. We couldn't tack across the channel because of its limited width; we were faced directly into the wind (no one can sail into the wind); the current was flowing out of the channel while we were trying to head in.

Out came the paddles as we lowered the sails. Paddling frantically in a futile attempt to clear the narrow cut, we began to tire. Each passing minute felt like an hour!

Since we could not get through on our own, we had no alternative but to drop an anchor and hope that a passing power boat would come to our rescue.

Time dragged by interminably and no other boat came into view. Apprehensively we pondered our situation and wondered what we would do if help didn't arrive. Would we spend the night in an open sixteen foot daysailer? Would it be advisable to swim to shore? Fortunately, those distressing speculations were soon dispelled when a small power boat appeared.

The skipper graciously took our tow line and we were soon clear of the channel and back under sail. The direction of the launch area finally offered a better tack and we were able to return to shore with no further problems.

Obviously, a small outboard motor would have to be added to our inventory before we attempted to explore further sailing areas.

# Disaster!!!

At last we arrived at the launch ramp, backed the car and trailer to the water and winched the boat upon it. It had been a long day.

Our usual operating procedure was to take the mast down while still on the ramp, but out of the water. However, that particular ramp was unusually steep, so we decided to drive to a more level place before working on the boat. When we drove back to the parking lot, we not only folded up for the day, but we folded up for the season!

Disaster struck!!! We had an incredible accident. No one saw the telephone wires strung across the entrance to the parking lot. Since that day we have read terrible stories involving high tension wires and sailboat masts, and we were indeed fortunate that those wires were not electrical.

When sailboat mast met telephone wires something was destined to give; not the wires, nor the mast. The whole forward deck of the boat peeled away from the hull and opened like a sardine can; and this, before we were even aware of the tragedy!

We gazed incredulously at the sight of the rigging firmly attached to the deck plates. We peered into the indecently exposed guts of the opened hull. We were aghast as we visualized the dollar bills marching end to end when the boat went for repairs!

In a state of shock barely holding back the tears, we drove home.

# As good as new . . .

The accident turned out to be embarrassing and expensive, but not fatal. After a series of telephone calls we managed to locate a boat builder with a good reputation for fiberglass craftsmanship.

We were so self-conscious at the thought of trailing our mangled daysailer, we considered doing it at night when her wounds would not be so obvious to all around us. However, we gritted our teeth, attached the trailer and bravely drove to the boatyard during the daylight hours.

It was a relief to learn that the repairs would not be as costly as we feared. When we picked up the boat before the next year's sailing season, we were amazed to see the superb job that had been done. Her scars were minimal and she was as good as new.

# The best of
# two worlds . . .

During the ensuing years, we became more confident and travelled farther afield. Trailing our daysailer without incident to many of New England's inland waters, we chose areas that also provided good campgrounds.

We had joined forces with our friends, Gloria and Dick, who owned a tent-trailer. The four of us enjoyed the best of both worlds with our vacations of camping and sailing.

Lake Winnipesaukee, New Hampshire, with its nearby campgrounds and interesting sailing areas eventually became our favorite locale. When the Mount Washington excursion ferry bore down on us, she appeared as large as an aircraft carrier and we hastened to get out of her way.

If the weather was good, we swam from the boat; but fair weather, or not so fair, sailing was a marvelous tonic after a hectic week.

Seldom was there a lack of wind. Often there was too much for our peace of mind, so we sailed within the confines of the harbors and bays. Occasionally, signs of an approaching squall would appear: dark clouds building in the sky, the wind freshening, the water surface becoming grey and choppy. We always hastened to return to the launching ramp.

The adage, "Don't sail in winds stronger than the length of your boat," was our guide. We didn't leave the harbor if the winds exceeded fifteen knots. Windy mornings seemed only to produce windier afternoons!

# **"Let me do it . . ."**

**20**

The combination of hot summer days, mountains, and a lake, create a pattern of shifting wind and rapid weather changes. Lake sailing is challenging because of the constant change in wind direction.

With our number one crew one day, we were making preparations to swim while anchored in the lee of an island when the familiar storm signs suddenly appeared. Two options were available: remain anchored on the quiet side of the island or raise the sails and return posthaste to our launch area.

Assuming that we could make it back before the impending storm, we prepared to sail. We hoisted the main, raised the anchor and I prepared to go forward to raise the jib. Gloria insisted on performing that chore so that she could prove her usefulness. As she stood on the bow to raise the jib, a sudden gust of wind heeled us to port.

One moment Gloria was standing on the deck, and an instant later she was sliding gracefully into the water. Fully clothed, her glasses in place, her new permanent undisturbed, she placidly treaded water while waiting to be rescued.

I consoled her and expressed my deep sympathy by saying, "But Gloria, I was the one who wanted to go swimming!".

# 21 Enter
# the Sailboat Fairy . . .

Our efficient crew came about quickly, lowered the main, put out the swimming ladder and retrieved our "man-overboard". Within minutes we were once again on our way.

The sky became blacker, the winds stronger and gustier, and the lake resembled the ocean. We were at the half-way mark, the point-of-no-return, when we took down the jib we had worked so hard to raise and decreased our mainsail surface by roller reefing.

We learned the hard way that our attempt to outrun the storm was foolish. Our inexperience and optimism had put us in a dangerous position. It was a "no-no". We should have anchored and waited things out.

The boat bounced and heeled uncomfortably and we became thoroughly soaked with rain and spray. What a miserable sail! The five miles or so seemed an interminable distance as the roar of thunder and flashes of lightning terrified us.

Our very own Sailboat Fairy must have looked after us that day as we returned to the safety of shore after our perilous voyage. Never again would we try to outrun a storm, if given the choice, unless we were no further than a half hour's sail from our destination. It is better to sit out a thunderstorm on the safety of an anchor than to risk capsizing in the middle of a large, deep lake!

## 22          **Of things mechanical**

With our number one crew, Gloria and Deck, we successfully sailed most of the lakes in New Hampshire and Maine. Those were happy years!

During a visit to our son-in-law's mother, Janice, in New London, Connecticut, we were fascinated by the many sailboats on the Thames River. It was an incentive to bring our daysailer on our next trip.

Some weeks later we did just that, and while Sharyn and Andy spent the morning ashore Janice joined us for a sail along the Thames. Plans were made to come ashore downriver and meet our children for a picnic lunch.

In order to sail down the river from the small boat launching ramp, we had to sail under a railroad drawbridge. The bridge is generally open during daylight hours unless a train is approaching. If the bridge is closed, a toot of a boat horn generally effects an opening.

The boat was rigged, launched and the trailer parked in our usual fifteen minutes. For convenience, we tried to start the outboard motor. Bob pulled and yanked, and though it seemed to cough a bit, the motor did not catch. We checked the fuel supply. Mechanical objects were, and still are, a source of wonder and amazement to us. After pulling a line or turning a key, we are helpless if the motor doesn't respond.

Subsequently we learned that small outboard motors tend to fill with sludge unless the gas petcock is turned off and the carburetor run out after each use. No one had ever thought to mention that procedure to us, and we had a gummed engine. Many times during the ensuing years, while motoring in circles to run out the gas, we have managed to crash into docks or be so far from our destination that we had to start all over again! However, running out the carburetor did seem to make a marked improvement in the performance of our motors.

Outboard or no, we cast off from the cove and proceeded according to plan. A perfect wind provided a fine sail downriver.

# 23                          A very
## late lunch indeed . . .

On schedule for our rendezvous with Sharyn and Andy we suddenly became aware of a change in the air. A haze had begun to develop and we noticed many boats coming upriver at that early hour. Did they know something we didn't?

As we rounded a bend in the river we saw the reason for the return procession. Fog, rolling up the river at a snail's pace, shrouded everything it reached in an impenetrable veil.

Quickly we came about to return to the launching site. To lessen the need for frequent tacks we tried to start the motor again. No luck.

We were making good time ahead of the fog until we were confronted with a closed drawbridge. From the number of boats tacking back and forth and blowing their horns, it was obvious that the bridge had been down for some time and there was no indication that it would soon open.

In company with the other boats we found ourselves sailing from side to side in the approaching fog while waiting for the cul-de-sac to disappear. Getting colder and hungrier, we sailed back and forth for almost an hour. Each minute seemed an eternity as we devoured our meager supplies.

Unable to anchor in that deep channel we had no alternative but to continue our boring operation while the fog crept inexorably towards us. Barely moving in the light winds, fearfully keeping a watch to avoid a collision, we finally heard, rather than saw, the train go by.

At last the bridge opened and we were able to return to the launch ramp. Several hours late, indoors, three hungry, cold and damp sailors enjoyed their picnic lunch.

# Virtue is its own reward . . .

While on vacation with Gloria and Dick we launched our boat though the day was quite windy. Discretion being the better part of valor, we did not venture from the protected confines of Meredith Harbor, Lake Winnipesaukee. Virtue was its own reward because the decision was fortuitous.

While we were sailing in the middle of the large harbor, the tiller suddenly felt disconnected from the rudder. It was! The fiberglass hinged bottom section of the rudder had parted from the top half. Tantalizing us, it bobbled on the surface for a minute or so and we tried to reach it. Trying to steer with just a paddle was difficult and we watched helplessly as the rudder gradually sank. By the time we considered diving in after it, it was gone. That was probably just as well since the lake was deep, the water cold, and the rudder weighty; not optimum conditions for that type of rescue!

When we examined our half-a-rudder, we found that the wing-nut on the hinge bolt had come off and the pin, holding the lower half of the kick-up rudder, had obviously worked its way out.

Dejectedly, we took the sails down, turned on the motor, and returned to the launch ramp. Where would we ever find a replacement rudder?

# 25 It must be a common accident . . .

Disappointment tends to give us an appetite, so we started our shopping expedition after first satisfying our hunger. Our plan was to canvass the various marinas for the sale, or loan, of a rudder. Once again our very own Sailboat Fairy was there, for we hit pay dirt on the third try!

At the Guilford Marina we located a used rudder which would fit our boat. It had been recovered from the lake and, although they did not wish to sell it, they offered to let us use it for the balance of our vacation.

When we returned home, a telephone call to the boat's manufacturer enabled us to order a new rudder. Unfortunately, the replacement took several weeks to be delivered, so our sailing season ended abruptly.

When our costly new mahogany rudder arrived, we realized that we had probably not been unique with our rudder-sinking episode. Unlike its fiberglass predecessor, the new wooden unit was designed to float.

Another lesson learned! Because wind and water cause considerable wear and tear, it is important to check all hardware, screws, hinges, halyards, sheets, everything on a regular basis.

# 26    The gas crunch and a new way of life . . .

For five years we had been camping and day-sailing. We were pretty fair campers, and Gloria and Dick were pretty good sailors. The big heavy cars we used for towing became a problem when the first of the gasoline shortages took place. Since we couldn't make a round trip to any of our favorite spots on one tank of gas, we always worried about fuel for our return. One weekend it was actually touch and go as we ran out of gas and were rescued by friendly police.

Since we live close to the ocean, it seemed a sensible idea to consider buying a larger boat that we could use in the ocean or trail. We visited boat shows and read advertisements.

We concentrated on twenty-two foot trailerable sloops. We didn't know then that the idea of trailering was not a practical objective. Operating on the assumption that the label "trailerable" was descriptive, we made another mistake.

Our requirements for that second boat were simple: a head, sleeping quarters for four adults and facilities to weekend aboard. What more did we need? What more we needed would take pages to list!

At one of the boat shows we were studying a trailer exhibit and chatting with the dealer. It was the end of the season and he offered us a very attractive package deal for his display twenty-two foot sloop and a trailer. We held a quick meeting of the board of directors and agreed to the sale.

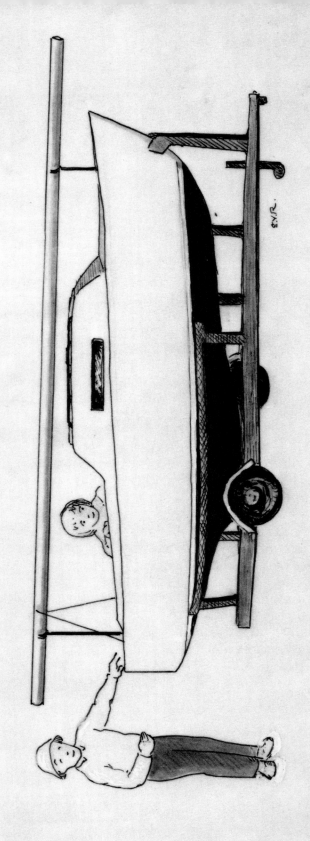

# 27    Boat number two . . .

With her tangerine hull, cabin berths for four, private head, sink, five gallon container for water and a table, she seemed a treasure to us. What luxury after an open boat!

We didn't notice that the forward berths accommodated only not-too-tall adults, or that the hull design had a high center of gravity. We were not cognizant of such details as hull shapes and stability. Another "no-no"!

Luckily for Gloria and Dick, they were eligible to continue as our number one crew since they could sleep in the V-berth!

The trailer was a beauty and had a two-speed winch that made it easy to handle the boat. At that time we expected to do a great deal of trailering. We arranged to take delivery ourselves, for, after all, we were expert trailer drivers and still owned a big, heavy car with towing springs and shocks.

When we took possession of our new boat a few weeks later, we began to have second thoughts about our plans to trail. After the initial sensation of size and weight (more than a ton hitched to us instead of a few hundred pounds) we managed nicely.

Still delighted with our purchase we drove home easily and uneventfully. When we backed the boat into the driveway it was with the assurance and expertise of five years' experience!

# 28     **A change of plan . . .**

Following the boat builder's instructions to attach the rigging, we found that we needed the strong muscles of our son David to help us step the mast. Because of its weight the mast was very difficult to balance and slot into the mast tabernacle.

It didn't take long to realize that we would have to make other arrangements for our boat and keep her rigging attached. Trailering would not be a good idea!

Because swimming in warm water is one of our pleasures we surveyed harbors south of Boston to find a place to moor. Mattapoisett Harbor, about sixty-five miles from home on the west shore of Buzzard's Bay, attracted us.

We attached no significance to the name "Buzzard's Bay" because it looked like a relatively safe place to sail. After all, the distance between points of land on either side was no more than ten miles, and it was even shallower than the lakes that we had sailed.

Renting a mooring at the Mattapoisett Boat Yard for the month of October gave us a chance to get acquainted with our new boat. The beautiful Indian Summer weather gave us no indication of the true nature of Buzzard's Bay.

It was another "no-no" that we never thought to ask anyone about general weather and sea conditions. Of course, we learned the hard way important details about Buzzard's Bay and its prevailing winds, choppy seas, fog and a well-earned reputation for meanness.

# Salt water sailing . . .

To improve our boating skills we started another course with the Coast Guard Auxiliary. We studied rules of the road, navigational aids, radiotelephone and so much more. As recommended, we purchased all the Coast Guard safety equipment and a VHF radiotelephone.

With our electric-start outboard engine, cooking and sleeping facilities and a roller-furling jib, we enjoyed our comfortable surroundings. When the aft hatch was closed our quarters were pretty tight. We became adept at moving about in a crouched position. After all, a low ceiling was certainly better than none at all!

Sailing primarily within the large harbor area of Mattapoisett, we practiced tacking and jibing and learned to pick up a mooring. Spending a weekend aboard was an exciting experience.

The light winds and calm seas were hardly a precurser for the future. The short days prevented our venturing far from the mouth of the harbor since we had to be back at our mooring in time for the last launch to shore.

# She must have a name . . .

Every boat in the harbor had a name; ours had only a state number. It was time to remedy that situation. We had managed to name two children without a problem, so what would be difficult about naming a boat?

As we spent days agonizing over each suggested name, it seemed that our boat was destined to be nameless. Numerous suggestions were offered and rejected. Loving parents had often called both mother and daughter "Sheina", a Yiddish word meaning "pretty one" and used as a term of endearment for female children. We eventually selected "Shayna" as an appropriate name for our new boat.

The day we affixed the six letters to her transom was exciting for us. After five years of having a nameless boat, we had now created an identity. As we prepared to attach the large white letters an identity crisis loomed. Was this to be Shayna I or Shayna II?

The decision was eventually resolved when we decided on Shayna II as a symbol of our improved status!

# 31     A navigational aid
# that disappeared . . .

When we returned from a sail and prepared to pick up our mooring, we discovered that we had managed another "no-no". Shayna II had been moored next to a bright yellow sloop, which we had used to locate our mooring. There weren't too many people sailing at that time of year, but the yellow sloop was gone.

With the disappearance of our "navigational aid", we found that we hadn't made sufficient provision to locate our mooring, and we didn't remember what it looked like. Although there were minor differences, all fifteen floats in the general area seemed identical.

Proceeding from mooring to mooring and hooking each pennant to study the name, we found it not only a tiring task but also a foolish one. Of course, ours was the fifteenth one!

Since that time we have learned to carefully scrutinize all landmarks and stationary navigational aids to get a positive fix on our location. It is easy to get confused in a sea of similar boats or moorings and the procedure is analogous to remembering where you put the car in a large, crowded public garage!

On our mooring at Mattapoisett we have attached a large, easily identified, plastic bottle to our pennant. It facilitates identifying our mooring.

# Tim-ber . . .

A dodger and sail cover were our first major investments during those early weeks. The dodger, a canvas awning extending over the hatch opening, allowed us to stand up in the cabin when the hatch was open. The sail cover protected the sail from the sun and sea.

That last week of October seemed unusually windy; but, as we later learned, not so unusual at all. The weekend arrived in style however: warm, sunny, calm; perfect for us to sail. As we drove along the waterfront admiring the picture-postcard view, we could not see our boat.

Our red hulled, gold masted, red sailcovered sloop, so easy to spot and identify, was not in sight. Perhaps the boatyard had changed our mooring. Butterflies fluttered in our stomachs!

We hurried to the launch dock, hoping against hope that we would be reassured. We weren't! There, lying on the dock, was a gold-colored mast, apparently ours. Careful scrutiny towards our mooring area revealed a red hull, bobbing on a mooring and looking strange indeed sans mast.

While we digested the shock of such a disaster, a boatyard worker explained the accident. Apparently, the turnbuckle holding the backstay came unfastened during the heavy windstorms. The mast toppled forward, hit the front deck, tore out the mast tabernacle and dented the front hatch. The launch crew discovered the accident and removed the mast before any further damage could result.

Another accident—another lesson! Turnbuckles should be taped, whether or not they have a locking device—which ours did not. So much to learn!

# The flying hatch . . .

After the abrupt finish to our sailing season we decided to bring the boat home for storage in the back yard. Without the mast to worry about, it was a simple matter to get the boat on the trailer. We were probably better drivers than sailors!

We made arrangements to return in the spring for repairs and a permanent mooring. Before driving home we picnicked by the water. After all, we rationalized, the damage was only cosmetic and the price of repairs seemed quite reasonable.

We were trailing the twenty-two on the highway when suddenly, we became aware of a car behind us, honking its horn and flashing its lights. After we pulled over to the side of the road the driver informed us that the front hatch of our boat had just flown away!

Another calamity! The other driver had seen our hatch soar through the air and come to rest on the grassy center strip some distance back.

Gratefully, we thanked the observant and considerate driver, prepared to find an exit, reverse direction, check our mileage and try to recover the errant hatch.

Our Sailboat Fairy must have returned for we located the hatch easily. It was reposing along the median none the worse for wear. How fortunate that it had not sailed into another car nor landed in the middle of the highway!

# 34

# We're very good at something . . .

During the cold winter months while waiting for the warm weather, we were cheered by looking out the kitchen window at Shayna II. We devised a simple door-type hook and eye to aid the existing hardware in keeping the hatch closed.

When spring arrived we hooked up the trailer and returned Shayna II to Mattapoisett. As we prepared to back the boat into an indicated slot between two others in the crowded boatyard, an employee offered to do the job for us. Little did he know that our driving was far better than our sailing!

Graciously, we refused the help, and, to the astonishment of the yard workers who were probably prepared for some entertainment, backed into the berth perfectly on the first try.

Once the repairs were completed, we waxed her hull, painted her bottom and prepared for the cruising season.

Anxious to improve our skills, we had joined the Coast Guard Auxiliary in order to participate in advanced classes. Lake sailing had been a challenge, but ocean sailing required more knowledge.

# At least this rudder floated . . .

Shayna II had not been in the water more than a few weeks when we managed another "no-no" and another accident. The winds had been brisk those weeks with what we hoped was unusual velocity. We learned soon enough that it wasn't so unusual.

As we boarded our sloop for a vacation weekend we found our rudder, looking a bit scratched and bruised, lying in the cockpit. During the week heavy winds and choppy seas had popped the rudder from its gudgeon and it had drifted ashore on a flood tide.

We had learned to keep all the screws tight, so the whole combination of tiller and rudder had remained intact. It was our good luck that it had happened during a flood tide and the rudder floated to shore instead of out to sea! Our accident-prone reputation was such that we were probably the first boat the sharp-eyed boatyard workers checked. A few cosmetic blemishes were the only consequences of that episode.

Another misfortune, fortunately minor, another lesson learned. How many more? We were told to tie the tiller firmly amidships to prevent the rudder from thrashing around in heavy seas.

# 36 **Our personal phenomenon of Buzzard's Bay . . .**

Although our studies had not yet included the intracacies and effect of ocean tides and currents, we knew enough to plan our excursions so that, whenever possible, our return trip would coincide with a favorable current. With a cruising speed between three and four knots, we were at the mercy of strong currents.

The season continued to be very windy. One lovely day when there was only a twelve knot breeze we were encouraged to explore beyond the confines of Mattapoisett Harbor. It was a smooth delightful sail as we crossed Buzzard's Bay on a perfect tack. In time, we turned around and headed back.

As we approached the entrance to Mattapoisett Harbor, we suddenly encountered the famous "Buzzard's Bay chop". In addition to the chop, each time at the hour of our return, we face a challenging sail. It is our personal phenomenon to head into the outer harbor at full hull speed and heeled well over in the churning seas.

The harbor may resemble a sea of glass before or after our arrival, but we always seem to precipitate a brisk wind.

# 37

# Rock and roll,
# sans music . . .

Trying to sail into the harbor that day was a frustrating experience. The shifting wind had placed the seas on our bow and we began to tack from side to side in an attempt to gain some distance past the harbor entrance.

After several tacks we realized that we had made very little forward progress. It seemed prudent to start the outboard motor. Without further ado, we pushed the button on our new electric-start motor. We pushed and we pushed! It was soon evident that if we couldn't sail in, we couldn't power in either.

After peering into the engine's innards, we fiddled with parts we could identify and probably some we couldn't. Nothing helped. What next?

As we continued to tack from side to side, the increasing wind swelled the seas. We mulled over our plight. Although we were only two miles from our destination, it seemed like ten.

Rocking and rolling in the rough seas was not our idea of fun. There had to be something constructive we could do.

# We take
# to the air . . .

Since the prospect of spending innumerable hours tacking back and forth in Mattapoisett Harbor didn't appeal to us, we decided that it was time to use our marine radiotelephone. After all, we bought it to use in case of an emergency, and this seemed to be an emergency.

When we radioed Mattapoisett Boat Yard no one responded. We reluctantly decided to call the Coast Guard. First, we rehearsed the radio lessons we had learned from the Coast Guard Auxiliary.

"Wood's Hole Coast Guard . . . Wood's Hole Coast Guard . . . Wood's Hole Coast Guard . . . this is Shayna II, WXZ 9-2-3-4 . . . over."

"Shayna II, this is Wood's Hole Coast Guard." How reassuring! We were not alone out there. We switched to a working channel and I explained our plight. They asked for a description of our boat, and then came an unexpected question. "What are your boat numbers?"

"M-S-2--uh---4--mumble, mumble," the numbers, which we knew by heart, had disappeared from our consciousness. I finally stammered, "Hold the line a minute." My answer was not proper radio procedure. "Stand by" is the conventional response.

Trying to read our registration numbers in the gathering dusk, we hung over the bouncing boat. Copies of the number were in our wallets, but the trauma had erased all such details from our minds.

# 39

# Anchor's away . . .

With our memory refreshed regarding our boat's registration numbers, we took to the air waves once again. We were told to put out an anchor while awaiting further instructions.

Anchoring should have been easy, but the anchor was reposing in the aft locker and Bob was determined to lower it over the bow. He should have lowered it from the stern and carried the line to a forward cleat. While we were rolling and pitching in the steadily increasing seas and drifting closer to the rocky shore, Bob was having difficulty manipulating the anchor.

What a fearful racket! I rushed from the cabin to find my husband wrapped in a hundred and fifty feet of anchor line including chain and anchor.

While Bob was trying to extricate himself from the web he had created, the Coast Guard called saying they had reached the boatyard by telephone and a tow was on the way. With the cacophany in the background, we probably sounded as if we were breaking up on the rocks, and they kept asking about our well-being.

"Do you have your anchor out?" they queried. I couldn't possibly tell them the truth, so I kept repeating that we were fine. Minutes later our rescuers arrived, and Bob proceeded to act like a man in the process of retrieving his anchor!

Ignominiously, we were towed to our mooring. We later learned that our engine was defective. Next project though, an anchor set on the forward deck and a rope locker into the forward berth. Not only would it be neater, but simpler, to drop the hook.

# **The rendezvous . . .**

Mattapoisett Yacht Club had planned a cruising weekend and we were encouraged to participate. A rendezvous at Red Brook Harbor on a Saturday afternoon was scheduled.

After an uneventful sail up Buzzard's Bay we entered the harbor, spotted some familiar craft and carefully proceeded towards them. Intending to raft, we suddenly found ourselves bearing down on our friends like a Kamikaze pilot! Despite our frantic attempts to reverse the engine and to steer in another direction, the boat had developed a mind of its own as it charged relentlessly forward.

The skipper of the boat on our collision course showed admirable qualities. At the last possible second Chet leaped over his life lines and with quick reflexes and strong feet he helped us prevent a collision by kicking our bow away.

How humiliating! No damage was done to either boat, but our egos were certainly battered. At that moment we would have preferred to sink, but we rafted with the group instead.

We later discovered that most of our steering problems were caused by a mast that could have fallen down and was seldom perpendicular to the hull.

# The race . . .

We joined the jolly gathering aboard the rafted boats and the group tactfully ignored our outlandish arrival.

While we were enjoying a second cup of coffee the next morning, a yacht club official came by and invited us to participate in a race back to Mattapoisett. Explaining that we were novices and had never raced, we declined the invitation. We were urged to participate, assured that our size was taken into consideration and given a one hour handicap.

Reluctantly, we agreed to join the group. As we headed for the starting line to get into position for the signal to send us on our way, our seamanship continued to deteriorate! We nearly collided with the committee boat and barely avoided cutting his anchor line. More steering problems.

To compound our discomfiture, in the scramble to avoid the official boat, Bob lost his hat, a not uncommon occurence. It sailed off his head and landed on the water where it didn't even have the good sense to sink. Most hats do.

Abashed, we tried to ignore the hat as it bobbed merrily on the surface. We probably would have lost something else had we attempted to retrieve it!

Our entrance and exit would certainly provide conversation for some time to come!

# 42

# A slow boat
# to Mattapoisett . . .

Our clumsy start, an omen of the balance of the sail, was certainly consistent with the prior day's dramatic arrival! Because it was our custom to sail close to shore where we felt more secure, four hours of sailing placed us in the lee of the land. We were drifting aimlessly with no wind to fill our sails.

As usual, when faced with a dilemma, we paused to munch our provisions. Should we break the rules and turn on the engine? We could remain becalmed for hours!

Suddenly our radio sang out, "Shayna II, Shayna II, Shayna II, this is Amulet . . ." Thrilled that someone remembered us, we acknowledged the transmission. Upon hearing that everyone was back at Mattapoisett, we turned on the engine to assist us in the unusually light wind.

When we finally returned to Mattapoisett, we learned that we had routed ourselves against the currents, had chosen a poor course in relation to the wind, and had sailed the farthest distance. At that point I determined to learn all I could about the intricacies of coastal navigation, tides and currents.

That autumn, I spent months studying with the Coast Guard Auxiliary. The course, "Piloting and Navigation", became a labor of love. When I heard that I was one of the few who had passed the arduous eight hour examination, Bob shared my sense of pride and accomplishment!

# 43

# So far, so good . . .

Exploring the lovely harbors in Buzzard's Bay kept us busy for weeks. If we found the winds too strong for our peace of mind, we stayed close to Mattapoisett Harbor. Sailing, dropping the hook, swimming, relaxing; we kept busy. We had bought a good swimming ladder to climb aboard.

At last, having acquired a moderate amount of confidence, we planned an expedition to Martha's Vineyard with Gloria and Dick. We chose the date to coincide with a favorable tide for passage through treacherous Wood's Hole. Since the tides did not favor a return passage through Wood's Hole, we planned to return by a longer route.

We crossed Buzzard's Bay easily, went through the Hole with sails filled and, just in case, with engine running. We anchored in Vineyard Haven Harbor early in the afternoon. Although it is possible to traverse Wood's Hole under sail alone, we never do so. The incredibly strong currents, rock stewn passage and tortuous channel are not to be taken lightly. We have heard many a call for help from the "macho" sailor who suddenly had found himself unable to negotiate the passage.

Our cruise that warm summer day couldn't have been more perfect.

# 44     **Thirty-twenty air-conditioning . . .**

Since this was our first trip to the Island, the next day we went ashore to do some sightseeing. The blistering heat, most unusual for the Vineyard, did not deter us.

While making arrangements at the tour office I naively inquired, "Are the busses air-conditioned?" "Yes Ma'am," replied the salesman, "We have thirty-twenty air-conditioning." As I looked at him quizzically, he continued, "Thirty windows open as we drive at twenty miles an hour."

After a hasty conference we decided to proceed with our planned tour. Bravely we boarded the tour vehicle, a yellow school bus, and squeezed into the seats. Enough togetherness, we took separate seats in a futile attempt to cool off. There weren't many tourists on that sightseeing trip!

The thirty-twenty air-conditioning wasn't at all effective and we could hardly wait for the sweltering ride to end. How we longed for the comparative coolness of the harbor! The charm and beauty of the Island were overlooked as our attention focused on the thermometers which read over one hundred degrees, an unheard of situation for Martha's Vineyard.

Back on the boat at last, we found it almost as hot as on shore.

# 45

# Red sails
# in the sunset . . .

Since we operate in a very democratic manner, we held a conference to discuss what we could do to escape the heat. The decision was made to pull anchor and sail elsewhere.

With more than four hours of daylight left we hoisted sail and took off towards Falmouth, Cape Cod. As we sailed leisurely across Vineyard Sound we could see the heat suspended over the land.

When the air became cool enough for sweaters within the hour, the soundness of our judgement was evident. With our shallow draft we were able to approach very close to shore to drop the hook. Here, too, shimmering over the land, the waves of heat were clearly visible.

Our anchorage, exposed to whatever stray breath of air there was, was comfortable. It was early to bed, early to rise, for we had a long sail ahead of us.

We didn't know then how very long the next day would be!

# 46

# A little boat in a big sea . . .

While polishing off a good breakfast and preparing to get under way, we checked the marine weather forecast on our radio. Sunny skies and light winds were predicted for the next twelve hours, perfect sailing weather for us!

Under a hot sun, through the sparkling seas, Shayna II slowly made her way while we relaxed and alternated at the helm. Crossing to Buzzard's Bay via Robinson's Hole, a narrow, shallow, but moderately calm channel, we added many miles to our return trip.

As we proceeded north towards Mattapoisett, we were oblivious to the insidious change taking place in the weather. Suddenly we couldn't help but notice the chill in the air and the choppy seas. Layers of puffy clouds began to darken the once blue sky.

Because we were making slow headway on a course that had become a beat, it seemed a good idea to turn on the motor. Although the United States Weather Bureau was still announcing fair skies and light winds, we could see that they were wrong.

As we started the engine, an approaching squall line became visible in the distance, and we became very conscious of our little boat in a big sea. The landfall for Mattapoisett about five miles away was the closest harbor. The current, caused by the oncoming waves, subtracted immensely from our forward progress which, at best, was about four knots.

# A freak accident . . .

47

Powered by mainsail, jib and outboard motor, we were wallowing through the seas. Suddenly, we stopped dead. Pandemonium broke loose! Actually, it was our engine that broke loose!

The bracket, together with the outboard, fell off the boat. To make matters even worse, the motor came to rest jammed between the rudder and the hull. This destroyed our steering. The motor hung by its battery cables to the boat.

There we were with our sails up, the engine wedged under the boat, the wind beginning to howl and the seas building to an uncomfortable height for a twenty-two foot boat.

With help from Gloria and Dick we quickly lowered the anchor and let out enough scope to hold our position. As usual, we were not that far from shore. Anchoring brought us into the wind which enabled us to take the sails down and restore a measure of safety and comfort.

Once the sails were secured we were able to assess our plight. Although the anchor seemed to be holding, we could see some large rocks much too close for comfort.

First things first. Bob and Dick attempted to retrieve the motor. Though they struggled valiantly, it was impossible. When we tried to use our radiotelephone we discovered that it was not operating. We learned later that the motor's dive into the water had disconnected all the battery terminals.

Our difficult circumstances were made more bearable by the presence of two nearby boats that had obviously seen our accident and were standing by.

# We anchor firmly . . .

One of the waiting boats was a small rubber speedboat which could not tow us. However, they asked the nearby fishing boat to call the Coast Guard for us.

After assuring us that the fishing boat had accepted our message, the folks in the small speedboat hastened to safety. Although the larger boat didn't offer a tow when they left, we assumed they had heeded our request to radio for help. We learned much later that they had not done so!

The squall struck, but we safely rode it out on our anchor. When again we attempted to extricate the outboard from its awkward position, we were still unsuccessful. When the worst of the storm was over, the fishing boat suddenly reappeared and offered to tow us to New Bedford. Since beggars can't be choosers, we accepted gratefully.

Once a tow line was attached, we began to retrieve our anchor. Bob and Dick struggled against the seas, but the anchor wouldn't budge. Because the fishing boat was anxious to leave, Bob cut our anchor line.

When the power boat started to tow us, it was apparent that we had another problem. Our fouled rudder was behaving like an anchor so we jettisoned our motor.

It was later suggested that we might have tied a fender or a cushion to the lines we cut to help retrieve the objects the next day. Of course, we might also have increased our loss by a fender or a cushion!

# The rescue . . .

Under tow only a short while, we suddenly stopped moving. The crew of the fishing boat appeared to be having problems of their own. It was soon evident that their engine had quit and now both of us were drifting.

At the end of a long tow line with no intermediary to act as messenger, we could only speculate as to what was happening. We were exhausted, but at least the storm was over.

About thirty minutes later we saw three power boats flying the flag of the Coast Guard Auxiliary. To us they appeared as knights in shining armor. We learned that they had just received the message describing our difficulties and had gone out again although they had signed off for the night.

Exhausted from our twelve hour sail and traumatic ordeal, we were delighted when Rick, one of our rescuers, a "rag-sailor" himself, offered to come aboard. He announced that he would help us sail into New Bedford Harbor. Timidly, we suggested that perhaps a tow would be quicker and easier for all concerned. Rick seemed insulted by that request and was anxious to prove that sailboats were self-sufficient. In the gathering darkness we wearily hoisted the sails and once again headed for port.

One of the rescue boats tagged along because we couldn't maneuver through New Bedford's hurricane gates without power. Too embarrassed to protest, we watched the power boat leave us once we were through the gates.

The day had taken its toll. It was completely dark, we were entering a strange harbor, we were so fatigued we could barely move or think. When we asked Rick if he would care to take the tiller, he was happy to do so.

# 50        Beyond
# the call of duty . . .

With a fresh skipper at the helm, the rest of us tried to gather our third wind; the second was long gone.

"There is something wrong with this boat! She doesn't respond properly!" suddenly pronounced our expert. Actually, that was rather a relief for us to hear since we had always presumed that the constant steering problems were due to our own ineptitude.

Our hardy and well-meaning rescuer had created a difficult state of affairs. We were at least a half mile away from the docking area, we had no power, no anchor, the boat could not be handled well enough to sail any further, and everyone else was long gone!

Undaunted, he attached us to a harbor buoy, climbed into our dinghy and started rowing to his marina. After an hour had passed and Rick had not returned, we began to worry that we might spend the night in the company of the buoy, out of food, water and patience!

At last, we heard the drone of an engine as our faithful knight reappeared with his own boat and a tow line. Above, and way beyond the call of duty, our Auxiliarist proceeded to help us unload four persons complete with paraphernalia. It was midnight in New Bedford when Rick packed us all into his Pinto and drove us to Mattapoisett.

# The silver lining to our cloud . . .

Since the prospect of sailing our boat to Mattapoisett did not appeal to us, we returned to New Bedford the next day with our trailer. It seemed prudent to haul the boat, examine her for hull damage, and try to discover why she handled so poorly.

We had just finished winching the boat on the trailer when Rick appeared. It was great to have another strong back to help with the mast. Once the mast was lowered the source of our problems was apparent. The mast tabernacle which held the mast in place on the deck was attached to the boat with two small screws, and one of them was loose enough to remove by hand! Later, we also discovered that the mainsail was too large and the jib too small!

Our disaster was a blessing in disguise, the proverbial silver lining. It would not have taken much more heavy wind or pounding seas to dislodge the mast. We were saved from a sailor's nightmare, being dismasted, by a freak accident! Our Sailboat Fairy was certainly watching out for us.

The hull had suffered no damage and we arranged to have the mast tabernacle through-bolted on the cabin roof. Additionally, we ordered a handmade, solid ash motor bracket to hold a new engine, and, of course, replaced all the other items that had been lost.

Another somewhat costly lesson was learned. At least no one had been hurt in what could have been a serious accident!

# Buzzard's Bay
# rolls again . . .

Fitted out and ready to cruise again, we invited friends to join us for a sail. If the winds were too strong or the seas too rough, we sailed within the large harbor area. On that day however, we were "promised" perfect weather for our small boat.

Under a cloudless sky the light winds propelled us across Buzzard's Bay to West Falmouth Harbor. Because the entrance is given to shoaling, only shallow draft boats were there. We never had to worry about hitting bottom with our twenty-two inch draft.

After enjoying a picnic lunch and swim it was time to return to Mattapoisett. As we left the protected harbor the day began to lose its earlier beauty. It wasn't long before Buzzard's Bay began to roll. As the seas heightened, our flat bottom smacked each wave with a sickening thud; our guests became apprehensive.

In addition to the unpleasant sound effects, the direction of the wind put us on a beat and we were not making much progress. In order to lessen our uncomfortable angle of heel we took down the mainsail, left the jib up, and turned on the motor.

Life jackets were placed in a handy position. Irene donned hers and we bravely chugged along keeping the bow angled into the waves. The roller-coaster effect of the seas was disagreeable and conducive to the bane of my existence, sea-sickness!

In retrospect, we believe that the "summer of our twenty-two" was the worst season for small boats that we have seen. Buzzard's Bay tended to get very rough and the winds, often quite strong and gusty, were unpredictable.

# 53

# We rival
# the
# "Perils of Pauline" . . .

Slogging along under power but a short while, we had another disaster. The vibrations of the motor, combined with the smashing seas, caused the outboard's clamps to slide off the new wooden bracket. Once more we were about to lose a motor!

It was a feat of gymnastics aboard the rocking boat for the men to catch the sliding motor and secure it with a line. The outboard's clamps should have been seated on rubber cups to prevent such an accident. It was impossible to make repairs while sailing, so we continued on our way while the men clutched the motor.

We experimented with both sails but found them too difficult to contend with in the heavy winds and rough seas. We attempted to shorten sail by roller-reefing, but with neither life lines nor safety harness it was impossible.

Although sailing with just the jib gave us the best performance, it was far from good. Since it would have taken us all night to return to our mooring, we eventually had to radio our boatyard for assistance.

Just as we thought that things couldn't be worse, they were! Another calamity was in the making. The "QE II" under full sail was bearing down on us from starboard. At least she looked the size of the "Queen" to us aboard our twenty-two.

We gazed in fascination as the beautiful forty-five foot sloop rigged with main and genoa sliced through the seas directly towards us. Barely moving on our beat, we were heavily disadvantaged, to say the least! We could not maneuver out of the other ship's way. Blinded by her own sails and oblivious to our presence, she bore down on us as we remained transfixed.

For what seemed an eternity we were all frozen to the spot. It couldn't be happening, it must be a nightmare, surely they would see us! Clasping the outboard motor the men were at the stern, wearing her life jacket Irene prepared to jump off the far side, discussing the option of using the radio I had one leg in the cabin.

Paralyzed with fear, we watched the sloop come closer and closer. The Sailboat Fairy must have come to our rescue once again for I emerged from my stupor in time to seize the air horn and get off a loud, prolonged blast.

The "Queen's" captain responded to the horn and gave his wheel a quick turn to port. The "Queen" passed our stern close enough to touch. With the hand that wasn't holding a glass he waved and continued on his way.

It was certainly time to call the boatyard and request a tow home!

# 55    **Onward and upward . . .**

One year of cruising Buzzard's Bay in a twenty-two foot shallow-keel, trailerable boat was enough to convince us that we had better advance our time table concerning a larger craft. We loved the area we had chosen to sail as it has warm water for swimming, many harbors to visit and a reasonable commuting distance from home. However, a larger boat was obviously a necessity if we intended to remain in Mattapoisett.

Since a bigger sailboat would constitute a major investment, we resolved to research the subject thoroughly. Our next boat would not be bought on the basis of price alone. We decided on non-negotiable requirements and shopped accordingly. We wanted twenty-eight to thirty feet, stand-up head room, heavy keel and stability, inboard power, as we had had enough of losing motors, and cruising facilities for five adults. In addition, we wanted a quality boat.

With those necessities firmly settled in our minds, we went shopping. We learned about hand laid versus blown fiberglass, through-bolted hardware, keel and rudder types, depth of foam rubber in cabin beths, storage areas, and length and width of bunks for sleeping. While negotiating the ladders from cockpit to cabin I became aware of the design of cabin steps. To me, many of the steps seemed hazardous.

The autumn months passed as we spent our weekends visiting New England's boat dealers.

One winter day when the temperature was near zero we were in Marblehead on our weekly boat shopping expedition. An enterprising salesman, recognizing a true prospect, for who else would be wandering around on such a beastly day, took us in hand. He showed us the Sabre 28. We could hardly believe our eyes for she seemed to fulfill all our requirments!

Filled with trepidation, we met with the financial expert and learned that one mortgages boats as one mortgages homes. We took careful note of all the statistics so we could assess our position.

Continued shopping expeditions compared all other boats to the Sabre 28. We called Sabre owners and heard "rave" testimonials about their performance. We were sold. Several weeks later, we made the commitment and ordered our boat. Some years afterwards, in Newport, Rhode Island, we met one of the owners we had consulted and assured him that we were happy we had followed his advice.

Our twenty-two with its new sails, trailer and all equipment, was put on the market and we were fortunate to find buyers immediately. They, too, were serious shoppers, for the day we met was bitterly cold and a snow storm was making life difficult. A completely equipped, sail-away boat was exactly what they had in mind and the sale was soon completed.

# Just plain
# Shayna . . .

Our shopping expeditions looking for equipment kept us busy and the winter months quickly passed. In addition to our more elaborate boat, we needed more elaborate accouterments. We bought: radiotelephone, swimming ladder, boom vang, stern barbecue, headsail furling system, anchors with chain and two hundred fifty feet of rode, docking lines, horseshoe life ring, six life jackets and countless miscellaneous items.

Since every master has his own idea of what constitutes a proper suit of sails, we discovered that larger boats seldom come equipped with sails. Remembering our incident involving the sloop blinded by its own low cut genoa, we chose to have our genny cut up from the deck to provide visibility ahead.

When we decided to document our boat we had to select a name. What a problem! Finally, we followed the path of least resistance and kept the name from our old boat. Since the new owners had chosen a new name, we were able to use "Shayna" once again. "Shayna III" seemed a bit ostentatious and we didn't find it necessary to proclaim an improved status any more. We settled for just plain "Shayna".

The most difficult part of the documentation procedure was the problem of parking a car in crowded Boston.

# 57    **If we could only fly . . .**

We knew that spring had arrived when we were notified that our boat was being shipped to a boatyard in Humarock for its sail-away preparation. Our weekends were busy as we rushed to complete all the necessary pre-launch requirements.

With tender loving care we painted each letter of her name, installed our radiotelephone and antenna and brought aboard some cans of food so that we wouldn't starve during our maiden voyage.

While working topside, one "not-so-pleasant" day, we managed our first "no-no" on the new boat. Because Shayna was on a high wooden cradle we had used a tall ladder to climb aboard. Suddenly, a nasty gust of wind toppled our ladder.

We appeared to be alone in the boatyard and at least eight feet off the ground. Of course, it looked twice that height from our position. Dismally, we peered over the side, but the thought of jumping to the ground was not at all attractive.

We scanned the area, whistled, yelled. We discussed the two options available: jump or wait. Neither choice appealed to us. As we stood in the cockpit trying to avoid making a decision, our Sailboat Fairy appeared in the guise of another human being. Again we called, whistled, yelled and finally managed to attract his attention.

When our rescuer arrived to replace the ladder, we learned another lesson. It is necessary to tie a line to a ladder so that it cannot stray. We've used many ladders these past years and always secure the ladder to the boat!

# Maiden voyage . . .

Despite some problems concerning the shallow channel out of Humarock and a last second repair of the sail slides, we started out one morning in May under cloudless skies, a ten knot wind, and a forecast of beautiful weather for several days to come. Accompanied by Barry, our yacht broker, we were in a state of bliss as we began the forty mile trip. She handled like a dream as we sailed a steady tack. It was more thrilling than we had anticipated and the miles flew by. We adjusted to the wheel steering quickly and learned not to hold the mainsheet. When Bob called, "Hard-alee", I could remain in place and not worry about the tiller punching me in the back!

We had sailed about twenty miles when we noticed that clouds were building in the sky. Since this is seldom a good omen we checked the weather stations once again and heard that fair weather was in store for us.

Although the wind had begun to freshen, there didn't seem to be any reason to abort our trip short of the Cape Cod Canal. Barry assured us of the dependability of our boat, so we elected to bypass the shelter of Plymouth Harbor in favor of continuing our voyage. Once again we experienced the unreliability of the National Weather Service which never did catch up to reality that day!

Perhaps, if we had had a barometer on board, we might have proven better weather forecasters than the experts. The cumulus clouds, the freshening wind and a falling barometer can be interpreted by an amateur! On our next shopping expedition we bought a set of weather instruments!

# 59

# This is really sailing . . .

As we sailed south on Cape Cod Bay it was reassuring to have an experienced skipper along. By the time we reached the "point of no return", the winds and seas presented a frightening picture to me.

"This is really sailing" joyously shouted Barry. The lee rail was awash and we were plunging through the turbulent seas. Personally, I wasn't quite sure that what we were doing was my idea of the epitome of sailing!

Despite the continued radio reports of fair weather we furled the genoa, reefed the mainsail and turned on the engine because the shifting wind had put us on a tight beat.

Our foul weather gear, more than adequate in the past, hardly kept us dry when large quantities of ocean sprayed the cockpit. Our next investment would be truly waterproof foul weather clothes.

The wind was howling, the seas were churning and splashing aboard and I was clutching the stanchions because I had visions of being swept overboard. Knowledgable, experienced Barry calmly announced, "When the wind blows the waves on board, it is blowing at least thirty knots, and when that water stings your face, it is blowing at least forty knots."

Since the water coming on board stung our faces, the knowledge of the force of the wind was hardly comforting to me! We had already put on our sun glasses to protect our eyes. They didn't help our vision since they were constantly obscured by salt water.

# Oh, how I suffered . . .

Pitching and rolling in the wind-whipped seas soon caused our large picnic cooler to slide around the cabin. We had forgotten about our built-in ice box, brought the cooler aboard and neglected to stow it securely. With each roll of the boat the heavy chest was slamming against our handsome teak interior.

Since Bob and Barry were busy sailing, reluctantly, I went below. Once in the cabin, unable to lift the cooler, I balanced it with my feet while desperately gripping the cabin hand rails. Trying not to look at the seas splashing the leeward windows, I stood there, feeling like a martyr, and suffered waves of seasickness.

Although I had downed a seasickness pill when the trip first became noticeably rough, the closed cabin, my uncomfortable position and the awful rolling, were torturous. Each minute seemed an eternity as I managed to swallow another pill.

In the midst of my misery, yet another emergency arose. The forward hatch popped open and the ocean began to splash into the cabin. I left my station as custodian of the cooler and moved forward to close the hatch. I felt the responsibility of the world resting on my shoulders! Did the men know what had happened? By the time I made it aft to inform them we could be flooded.

As the boat lurched through the high waves I desperately tried to reach the hatch. In the midst of my ineffectual efforts, Bob suddenly appeared, grasped the offending cover and pulled it shut.

First order of business before sailing again would be to attach a simple door-hook-type closure to prevent such an accident.

Bob was able to move the ice chest and I joined the men in the cockpit. The cold, the wet and the stinging spray, were all still preferable to being below. We pumped out the bilge as we slowly sailed to The Harbor of Refuge at the east end of the Cape Cod Canal. We had had enough sailing for one day!

## 61                                Terra firma, at last . . .

The one redeeming feature of that interminable trip was the knowledge of how well our boat handled. During the last ten miles, which took us three and a half hours, the propeller was often out of the water and we exceeded the builder's recommended twenty-six degrees of heel by quite a bit. Once inside the Harbor of Refuge we breathed great sighs of relief.

After we had tied to the dock and happily placed our feet on terra firma, the friendly harbormaster welcomed us. What a picture we must have made! We were drenched to the skin, chilled to the bone, and I, a bilious shade of seasick green. The Harbormaster brought us a small electric heater and invited us to his warm quarters for hot coffee.

As we thawed out we learned that the winds had been clocked over forty-five knots and the weather bureau was in the process of revising the forecast to warn of several days of inclement weather.

There we were in Sandwich, cold, wet, tired and hungry, with one car in Humarock and another in Mattapoisett. It seemed sensible to go home since we couldn't sail for several days. Once again the harbormaster came to our rescue by suggesting that we ask the Captain of a fishing boat due in shortly for a ride to Mattapoisett.

Eventually, Bob got a ride to Mattapoisett and returned to pick us up.

After that, three lobster dinners did wonders for our morale.

Shayna's sea-kindly performance during that gale has served to reassure us during the years when we have been caught in disagreeable weather. In retrospect, it wasn't such a bad experience after all!

# 62    We sail in the middle now . . .

When the weather finally cleared several days later, Bob and I returned to the Harbor of Refuge to complete our trip. Because of the strong, up to five knots, current which is caused by the very different tide ranges at the east and west ends of the Cape Cod Canal, passage under power is required and a favorable current is advised.

Although we had viewed the Canal from shore many times it was an exciting and different perspective from the water. Powering along with the current, we made an easy transit.

We raised the sails for the last leg of our journey. Joyfully we tacked and jibed in order to become familiar with our boat. It was a perfect day and we were bursting with pride when we entered Mattapoisett Harbor several hours later.

Each weekend we lived aboard and cruised to nearby harbors. The realization was even more exciting than the expectation! Our five to six knot cruising speed was a revelation and we discovered the joy of sailing in the middle of Buzzard's Bay! No longer did we hug the shore!

# 63

# Our first grounding . . .

While visiting our friends Winnie and Ted in Onset one weekend we made a careless mistake. Unmindful of the tide range we tied to Ted's mooring during a high tide and dinked ashore. When we returned, several hours later, it was obvious that our almost five foot draft Sabre was resting upon the bottom.

The mooring area, deep enough for large power boats, was too shallow for us. Since we had neglected to consult both the tide book and our own depth sounder we were surprised to discover that low tide left us sitting on the mud. It was another "no-no".

When we transferred the Captain and our guests to the forward starboard side the boat heeled just enough to raise the keel off the bottom. Fortunately, we were able to start the engine and back the few yards needed to reach a more suitable depth.

We've been told that you can't be a sailor until you have experienced a grounding, and we have managed it several times. Some easy ways to get off the bottom are to raise as much sail as possible to heel the boat, to wait for an incoming tide, or to hail a power boat for a tow. There are other more difficult alternatives.

However, grounding is always a "no-no"!

# 64

# All's well that ends well . . .

Just as we were beginning to hope that our sailing expertise was beyond the novice stage, we discovered that we had done another "no-no". After spending the weekend at Cuttyhunk Harbor, we prepared to return home. Despite indications of heavy weather beyond the protection of the harbor, the forecast did not presage anything unusual. After all, we had weathered a gale unscathed and were not worried about a little extra wind.

Our sail inventory was minimal, a mainsail with one set of reef points and a one-twenty-five genoa with roller furling. Since the direction of wind and seas dictated a run, we elected to sail with just a reefed mainsail.

Once clear of the island we found ourselves practically planing over the high rolling waves which made steering difficult. Though our boom vang was attached to prevent a jibe, I found the trip a frightening experience.

We had too much sail up for the wind and sea conditions, but were unable to reef any further and so we had no choice but to endure our roller-coaster ride.

Considering the twenty-some miles involved, we were abreast of Mattapoisett Harbor in record time. However, the high rollers prevented us from making a turn into the harbor because we were afraid of broaching, so we sailed right on by! We were able to angle towards shore at last and finally come about in the shelter of the land. Even though we had overshot Mattapoisett by three miles, we were soon safely on our mooring.

After spending thousands of dollars on a boat we had foolishly economized on our sail package. We ordered a small headsail immediately and added a second set of reef points to the mainsail. We have since used the storm jib innumerable times and the second set of reef points twice!

# 65    A nocturnal swim . . .

In order to get an early start Saturday morning, we try to arrive at our boatyard Friday evening about supper time. On Saturday we thus avoid the line of boats awaiting their turn at the dock for gas, water or ice.

It was late in the season when dusk is early, and we were rushing to perform our chores so we could proceed to our favorite anchorage across the harbor before total darkness set in. In record time we had managed to stow our provisions, fill the water tank, buy and load the ice, park the car and cast off from the dock.

In the semi-darkness as we powered across the harbor the engine suddenly gurgled and stopped. Fortunately, we were out of the mooring area and not in any danger. However, the engine would not start again. When Bob came aft to lend his support he suddenly discovered the answer to the mystery. In our haste to leave the dock he had neglected to pull aboard all the docking lines and the forward one had trailed into the water and wound itself around the propeller. That is another "no-no".

We couldn't stay where we were in the middle of Mattapoisett Harbor. We could hoist the sails, or go for a swim; actually, only one of us needed to swim. Since the swim seemed to be an eventual necessity, Bob opted for a nocturnal dip. Fortunately for him the water temperature was a comfortable seventy-five degrees, though the air was much colder. How lucky he was that it hadn't happened in the frigid waters further north!

A quick plunge in the balmy sea enabled Bob to untangle the docking line from the propeller. It took longer to let out and retrieve the anchor than it did to free the prop. Two lessons learned that time: always check the mooring lines and shift the engine into neutral at the first sign of any problem.

# 66

# The errant sail . . .

During that first season with our Sabre we had a problem with our roller-furling genoa. In all but the lightest winds the furling drum would invariably jam and it prevented us from rolling in the large sail. Bob would have to go forward and manually wind the genny while I struggled to head the boat into the wind and man the furling line. Something was wrong; the greater the wind, the more difficult the procedure.

One "too-much-wind-to-sail day" we brought the boat to the dock to remove the furling line and, in an attempt to prevent the jamming, substitute a lighter one. Bringing the original line with us to compare heft and length, we made our purchase at the Yard store. So that we wouldn't tie up dock space, we motored toward our mooring to effect the repair. Our good intentions were not rewarded with a good result. We did another "no-no".

We were about two hundred feet away from the dock when a gust of wind caught the clew of the furled, but unattached-at-the-bottom genoa and unrolled all two hundred and twelve square feet of dacron. Heavy winds caused the sail, with a mind of its own, to flail about the deck and billow over the water. Because the bad weather had discouraged boating, the harbor was full of moored boats.

Blinded by the sail, surrounded by boats, we were in another idiotic predicament. The heavy winds and rough seas created quite a challenge as Bob pursued the sail which was whipping from port to starboard and starboard to port. With a flying tackle he finally managed to bring the sail to the deck while just barely remaining on board himself!

During this exhibition I was busy leaping from the port to starboard seats to catch a glimpse of the surroundings and steer away from the other boats. It was so embarrassing. We regretted the day we painted her name in such large, legible, bright letters. We wished we were anonymous.

The Sailboat Fairy must have been with us again, for the only damage was to our dignity. When we purchased a better quality furling drum, the problem was solved.

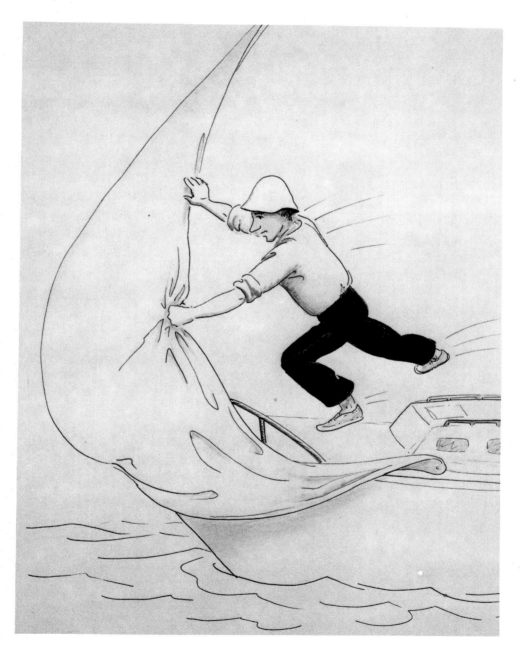

# Hoist on our own . . .

If given our "druthers" we prefer a floating pier, although one is not always available. One day at the Onset Bay Marina we learned a great lesson on how not to dock.

After checking the tide tables we had allowed several feet of line for the fall of the tide. Bob is super tidy about attaching lines, so we were thoroughly fastened to the dock with bow, stern and spring lines properly knotted and cleated. We didn't notice that it was a time of the spring tide, a peak of high and low tides during the month. Everything looked shipshape when we returned to the boat after a pleasant evening with Winnie and Ted.

During the wee hours of the morning, a gentle creaking sound began to penetrate my consciousness. Certainly more asleep than awake, I tried to ignore it. It didn't go away and Bob didn't waken. Reluctantly I arose and peered through the forward hatch.

A shocking sight instantly broke my somnolent state. With the bow pulpit caught on the pier we were hanging from the dock by our own docking lines. My cry of horror quickly brought Bob to attention. He managed to get off the boat, not an easy thing to do under the circumstances, and release the lines. All those tidy fastenings plus the weight of the hanging boat made it a difficult chore. The shame of our foolish plight and the need for silence at that ghastly hour were additional burdens!

At last, the lines were released and we settled into the water. To our relief, we had caused no damage to either the dock or our boat. Our Sailboat Fairy was certainly working overtime on our behalf.

# When west becomes north . . .

During our second season with Shayna, after vacationing at Nantucket with Gloria and Dick, we started sailing towards home. Although the winds were too light, it was pleasant. After a while the wind became stronger, a not unusual occurence, and we rather enjoyed the accelerated movement after our hours of inactivity. The weather forecast, per usual, was still telling of gentle breezes; but we knew better.

The weather continued to deteriorate, the increasing seas sprayed aboard and the shifting wind placed us on a beat. We shortened sail, turned on the engine and carefully followed our plotted course from buoy to buoy. At last, the landmark, Cape Poge Lighthouse in Edgartown, came into view.

We were about six miles off the coast, but our plotted course following the navigational aids would add another mile or two. Making slow progress against wind and current, we were all tired, wet, cold and hungry. Consulting our chart to see if we could take a short cut to the Vineyard, we determined that a diagonal course would be safe. At that point we managed another "no-no", and a dangerous one at that!

With the lighthouse as a target, we steered the boat at it. Inexcusably, we didn't follow a compass course, nor determine the set and drift of the currents. We changed helmspersons often because the flying spray made steering exhausting. We should have been sailing almost due west, but we were actually sailing north; and no one noticed!

When I took my turn at the wheel, I suddenly focused on the compass; and, at the same moment, became aware of peculiar churning seas on our port side. Hastily, we turned on the depthsounder, something we should have done earlier in such treacherous waters, and discovered that something was wrong. To our horror, the light barely hit the six foot reading! Quickly, we made a ninety degree turn to face away from the breaking seas to give us time to study the chart.

Chagrined and horrified at our stupidity and overconfidence, we pored over the chart to discover our error. We had neglected to consult the tide book illustrations which showed a strong southerly current between the two islands at the time of our passage. The current had drawn us south, towards the shoals, while we thought we were heading west towards the lighthouse.

With depthsounder on and chart in hand, we carefully threaded our way through the treacherous rocks and managed to arrive in Edgartown nine hours after leaving Nantucket! Another lesson learned the hard way. Our Sailboat Fairy must have watched over us once again!

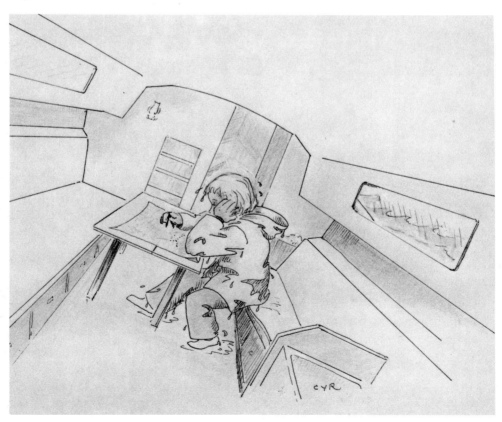

# 69 Boomps - a - daisy . . .

It was almost dark when we finally entered Edgartown Harbor. The usual anchorage area was "wall-to-wall" boats as we powered around looking for a spot to drop the hook. Rather than weave through the busy anchorage in the dark, we joined three boats that were anchored on the opposite side of the channel.

After putting down the customary sixty feet of rode, we remembered to check the depthsounder. We managed to avoid another blunder when we added eighty feet of line because the depth was twenty-five feet instead of the usual twelve. Finally, we went below to provide ourselves with some well-deserved, maybe not really deserved, but certainly needed, refreshments.

However, tranquility did not last long, for, about ten minutes later, we felt and heard a thump on the port side. Hastily, we scrambled topside and found ourselves nestled cosily against a large shallow-draft boat. When last seen, said boat had been far away indeed.

Her Captain informed us about the unusually strong currents in that anchorage area and suggested using fenders and even more anchor rode. We didn't discuss who had drifted into whom, although it was our opinion that our heavy keel was not the offending boat; we followed his suggestion and added another thirty feet of scope. We could then understand why one side of the channel hosted two hundred boats and our side only four!

On a visit to Menemsha we found the harbor full and had to anchor along the bight outside of the breakwater. Since the tides were wrong to make the trip up the channel to Menemsha Pond there were several boats in the same predicament. We let out enough scope to anchor in the eight feet of water.

Although it was a beautiful quiet evening, the anchorage was not calm. The prevailing winds were apparently responsible for the constant stream of rollers that caused the boat to rock incessantly. I praised the creation of seasickness pills as I finally managed to get to sleep.

Rudely awakened by a vicious thump during the wee hours, we rushed topside. We gazed incredulously at the fancy sloop noisily crashing into us. There wasn't any doubt about who moved into whom!

"Let out some more scope," shouted the other skipper. "We have plenty of line out now, how many feet did you lay out?" I asked. "One hundred and fifty feet," proudly announced the nuisance. "In eight feet of water!" We were appalled. His anchor line was probably around, about and under us a half a dozen times. At one o'clock in the morning no one was in the mood to try to unravel the mess, so we did the only sensible thing, we rafted together.

It was agonizing to lie there, tied together, bumping and grinding as each roller lifted us at different intervals. Frantic from the constant clatter, we finally suggested taking the other boat's anchor line on our cleat. It was a slight improvement.

Until that night we had always found our fenders more than adequate, but our next purchase was to be two, huge fenders! Of course, the offending boat had fenders the size of doughnuts and they were about as helpful.

Eventually, the long night was over and we were able to free ourselves from our albatross!

# 71

# Power boats are nice to know . . .

With our number one crew along we experienced yet another episode of injured dignity. We had spent the Fourth of July weekend in Edgartown and, heading for home, we powered out of the harbor. As we turned the boat into the wind to hoist the sails, our attention focused on the tell-tales. Such was our concentration while raising the sails, we failed to notice that we had strayed beyond the channel boundary.

With the mainsail up we prepared to sail, but the boat didn't respond. It didn't take long to discover that we had grounded!

When we took stock we could see that we had a problem. Because the tide was going out our situation would worsen before it would improve; there was not enough wind to heel the boat and raise the keel; and there didn't seem to be another boat around. Anxious to get started for the long trip home, we decided to radio for aid instead of attempting any of the various time-consuming alternatives.

Trying to call the Edgartown Harbormaster on the radio was a project in itself. It was almost impossible to get a "word in edgeways" through the continuous calls. Finally, a boat named Sea Flite answered our call and graciously offered us a tow. While awaiting our release, we heard the Edgartown Harbormaster calling us on the radio. We explained our plight and added, "We are a twenty-eight foot sloop, I didn't ask Sea Flite its size." "We are a thirty-eight foot power boat," boomed over the radio.

In a short while our rescuer arrived, attached a tow line to the port cleat, positioned the crew on the starboard side and carefully backed us off the shallows. Sea Flite was most competent and we were most grateful.

# 72

# Caution creates its own crisis . . .

With the sails beginning to fill we were on our way at last following a course from buoy to buoy. Despite our beat and an unfavorable current, as strong as three knots, we were reluctant to turn on the engine and spoil the tranquility of a pleasant sail.

Straying a bit from our plotted course because of the direction of the wind, and mindful of our recent grounding, we turned on the depthsounder and assigned Gloria the task of watching it. About a half hour after our last fix Gloria suddenly shouted, "It's getting shallow!" "How shallow?" I asked. While relaxing in the cabin she had turned the instrument around and was reporting, "Twenty...fifteen...ten..." "Impossible," I thought, as I tried to sight the bottom over the side. Panic reigned there in the cockpit as we all read the depthsounder. Fulfilling my position as navigator I instructed Bob, "Turn towards the Vineyard while I study the chart." The shoal areas were towards the mainland, so a course back towards the Vineyard had to be safe.

After studying the chart, I reported, "We just have to be in over sixty feet of water." The light suddenly dawned! We were in over sixty feet of water - sixty...plus twenty...fifteen...ten. It was deep enough to use the fathom scale on the depthsounder. Gloria had missed the progression from fifty to sixty to the second time around the dial. Our cruising area is generally so shallow we seldom read the depth in fathoms.

No crisis after all; what a relief!

# Ripped off . . .

Hadley Harbor, a large, peaceful, hidden harbor between Nonamesset and Naushon Islands is not well marked on the charts. The easiest way to find it is to follow any sailboat that seems to be turning southwest from the Buzzard's Bay side of Wood's Hole. Lacking a leader, look for a small can and nun which mark the harbor entrance. Nearly a hundred boats enjoy this beautiful harbor most weekends.

Although the shore is private, swimming, bird-watching and dinking provide ample entertainment. We have explored, by dinghy, many of the passages leading to Buzzard's Bay and Vineyard Sound. We have fed the beautiful Canadian geese, who have even taken food from our hands, an assortment of ducks and ducklings, but have developed an aversion to the sea gulls.

During one of our weekends at Hadley's, Bob was cooking some luscious-looking steaks on the stern barbecue. When he turned to admire a pair of wild geese, a brazen gull swooped down, snatched a steak and flew off with it. He took the larger one, too!

Bob has learned to keep a weapon handy be it a mop or tongs, so that he can guard the grille from predators!

# The morning after the night before . . .

One morning, after an unexpected nighttime thunderstorm had brought heavy rainfall to our anchorage, we saw that a neighboring boat had done a "no-no". The unfortunate skipper had left his outboard motor attached to his dinghy and enough rain water had accumulated to dunk the outboard in the salt water. This is not recommended treatment for motors; they seldom work after a salt water bath.

While our neighbor was bailing his dinghy and trying to rescue his motor, he capsized the dinghy. Since he was wearing his life jacket he was in no personal danger. Eventually, the poor fellow managed to get the dinghy afloat and the motor aboard his sloop.

Our inflatable dinghy, too, was filled with water but firmly attached to our boat; and the outboard was positioned at its place on our stern rail. After congratulating ourselves on our foresight in removing the motor, we were chagrined to discover that we had managed a "no-no" after all.

Our plastic oars had apparently blown, or floated, their way to oblivion, since they were no where to be found. We couldn't go far in a dinghy without oars. With our luck concerning engines, to be without oars was unthinkable!

# 75

# Skill is
# its own reward . . .

Although Bob can read a chart or plot a course, I take charge of our navigation. We have found that a division of responsibility is efficient and convenient for us.

We have learned that fog seldom arrives without warning. First there is haze, then mist, then fog that thickens and obscures the landscape. While sailing on a hazy day we have had a curtain of fog drop and envelop us.

Although it is difficult to sustain a constant speed while under sail, we follow our compass, estimate our speed, watch the time and compute the distance to our next navigational aid. When our calculations tell us we should be in the vicinity of a marker, we carefully listen for the expected gong, bell or whistle. As yet another guide to our position we monitor the depthsounder.

While on vacation with Gloria and Dick we were overtaken by a thick fog off the Rhode Island coast. Under power, because there was no wind, we were all maintaining a constant watch and sounding our fog horn at regular intervals.

The sounds from the Watch Hill Lighthouse, plus the chime of a nearby bell, were heard right on schedule. Not on the agenda however, was a rather deep horn which seemed to be getting louder and closer. Nervously, we continued to toot our own horn as we heard the oncoming wail, heralding the approach of a large ship, intensify.

Within minutes, the deep blast of a fog horn came, and went. Only the great wake of the large vessel, which passed us unseen, gave proof of its presence.

One day, when I was able to question a Coast Guard officer about the effectiveness of the radar reflector we use in our rigging during periods of poor visibility, I was assured that they are of inestimable value to a radar operator. It was obviously effective that day when we never saw the ship that passed us in the fog.

# 76

# An unconventional way to moor . . .

In addition to my duties as navigator I handle the boat under power when docking, anchoring, or picking up a mooring. With our division of responsibilities it seemed logical that Bob would be the one to drop the anchor, retrieve it, jump off the boat when arriving at a dock, jump on the boat when leaving a dock, spear a mooring with the boat hook and do all the tough physical chores. While he is managing those tasks I stand at the wheel and use the engine to expedite matters. Generally, now that we have had several years of practice, we manage all those maneuvers with superb style!

Our mooring seems to be in the middle of a very crowded area. When we come in to pick up our pennant there is not much room to maneuver among the boats. When powering this presents no problem, but when sailing, it is intimidating. In order to pick up our mooring while under sail, we start with two strikes against us: the phenonemon of the increased wind and seas and the problem of reversed responsibilities. Bob is better at handling the sails which leaves me the job of grabbing the mooring.

One day we decided to try to improve our mooring skills under sail. As Bob turned the boat into the wind I deftly speared the mooring line but we continued to move. I had to make a quick decision: drop the mooring or join it in the water. Because I didn't have the strength to hold the pennant against the forward drift of the boat, I chose to drop it.

Suddenly there was a thump, and we came to a sudden halt. We had managed to hang ourselves on our own mooring - another "no-no", of course. Backwards from all the other boats with our rudder entangled in the mooring line, we were in another idiotic predicament.

The recriminations were short: "You could have held the line." "You should have stopped the boat." We concentrated on a solution. Rocking the boat from side to side, jabbing the water with the boat hook, in some miraculous way we managed to free ourselves in a remarkably short time. The Sailboat Fairy must have been watching over us once again.

Sometime later we watched another poor soul make the same mistake only he suffered a worse fate. Unable to free the boat, he climbed into his dinghy and capsized the dinghy before he managed to release his boat.

# Our blunders become more sophisticated . . .

With Gloria and Dick along once again, in light southwest winds we were cruising from Cuttyhunk to Newport. Although our course was a beat, a favorable current was a great help. When the wind increased a couple of hours later, we sailed even faster.

Entirely unpredicted, the wind became stronger and the steadily worsening seas became a nuisance. We donned our foul weather jackets and were considering the addition of trousers when the whole thing became academic. A large wave crashed aboard and instantly soaked the four of us.

We had been warned of fish traps in the area and had carefully plotted our course to avoid them. In the rapidly deteriorating weather, we furled the genoa, started the engine and slogged our way towards Newport.

Suddenly to our horror, we discovered that we were encircled by a fish net area. Another "no-no!" The large red balls fencing us in for miles were not a happy sight. How we arrived in the middle remains a mystery to this day. Because the high waves and flying spray hindered our vision, oblivious to what was happening we must have sailed over the perimeter of the nets on a wave crest.

Circling inside the trap and searching in vain for an opening, we had no choice but to try to sail back out. We set our course to a broad reach so that we would have maximum speed, shifted the engine to neutral to stop the prop when we reached the trap line, and held our collective breaths. The Sailboat Fairy must have been watching over us once again, for we sailed out of the fishnet area without getting caught.

# We develop a sixth sense . . .

When we left Newport for our next port of call we were in unfamiliar waters. The day was calm and we sailed and powered the short distance to Point Judith.

Upon reaching the Point Judith Harbor of Refuge we followed the suggestions mentioned in our cruising guides and continued through the channel towards the pond. The passage was difficult to recognize and we carefully monitored the depthsounder while we looked for someone to question. At last we saw a fisherman aboard a docked fishing boat and requested anchoring advice. He suggested that we drop the hook about a thousand feet ahead.

Perhaps we were beginning to develop a sailor's sixth sense for we chose to ignore his advice. Although there were a couple of small power boats anchored where the sailor had pointed, we like to be among our own kind. Disregarding the recommended anchorage we soon saw a small cove which hosted several moored sailboats and an empty mooring, too. Happily, we hooked the free line and spent a pleasant night.

In the morning, which coincided with low tide, we discovered that we had managed to avoid another grounding. The anchorage we had not used appeared to be about two feet deep.

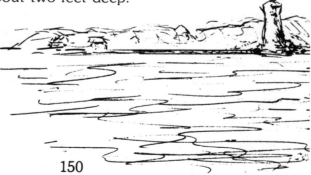

# 79 Where cope is the name of the game . . .

Shayna smartly entered the Thames River channel from Long Island Sound and we thrilled to the memorable experience of sharing the passage with several Navy submarines. What a difference six years had made! The last time we sailed the Thames River in New London was in our sixteen foot sailboat. Once settled at a dock we had an opportunity to take care of our laundry and restock the larder.

New London was our half-way point and we changed crews. Gloria and Dick returned home while Sharyn, Andy and Janice signed on for the return voyage. When we left the next day and began the short trip to Stonington, the weather was sultry and still. On a run, with the whisker pole holding the genny, we slowly sailed "wing and wing".

Before long it began to look like rain. As the sky continued to darken I remembered my soaking some days earlier and went below to don my foul weather gear. Our passengers joined me moments later and announced that it was drizzling. Comfortably attired in my foul weather gear I started up the cabin steps to relieve Bob at the wheel. One look at the sky and I was aghast! I saw Bob, looking like the Al Capp cartoon figure, Joe Bfstyczk, with his own private rain cloud hanging over his head.

"Get the whisker pole out of the genny!" I shouted. Without a moment's hesitation Bob sprang into action. Just as he made his way back to the cockpit to reel in the genoa, the storm struck. The boom vang on the mainsail prevented a jibe and Bob furled the large sail. I had started the engine and was watching the tell-tales to steer the boat into the wind.

151

The heavy downpour...the swirling wind...our world consisted of those few square feet where we tried to keep our balance and steer our boat. During those frantic moments we spun about and lost track of our heading. The squall was over as quickly as it began and we found ourselves facing the opposite direction but otherwise unscathed!

What fortuitous timing! The few minutes warning afforded by the sight of the ominous black cloud swooping down from the rear undoubtedly saved us from disaster!

# Epilogue

Although there are probably an infinite number of "no-no's" waiting to be encountered and catalogued, we feel that we have done our share of testing. Hopefully, we have learned our lessons well so that we will be competent and knowledgeable when a crisis occurs.

Mother Nature and her consort King Neptune are powerful forces. They deserve our utmost respect. Overconfidence can lead to trouble; carelessness can lead to disaster. The learning process never ends.

From the peace and serenity of a quiet anchorage at sunset to the effort and stress of fighting eight foot seas and gale force winds, sailing spans a gamut of emotions.

We hope the Sailboat Fairy will continue to appear at propitious moments.

May all our seas be calm;
may all our winds be fair;
may all our tides be favorable!

# A glossary of terms as used in this text

Points of sailing: 1) running
                     2) beating—pointing
                     3) reaching

1) Running: the wind comes from a direction behind the boat causing the boom with the mainsail to extend out from the boat at a right angle to the hull. The headsail may be extended on the other side of the boat, "wing and wing".

2) Beating: the opposite of running; the wind blows towards the bow of the boat and the sails are pulled tightly to the center. Beating causes the greatest amount of heel compared to other points of sailing.

3) Reaching: the fastest point of sail; the wind blows to the side of the boat. Reaching is every point of sail that is neither running nor beating.

Rigging the boat: 1) stepping the mast
                     2) shrouds
                     3) fore and back stays
                     4) spreaders

1) To step the mast is to raise it from a horizontal to a vertical position and fasten it to the deck in a fitting called a mast tabernacle.

2) Shrouds are wires from the mast that attach to the deck on each side of the boat and support the mast.

3) Fore and back stays are the wires that run from the mast to the bow and stern and support the mast.

4) Spreaders are braces that extend horizontally from the upper part of the mast and have the shrouds run through their tips.

Sheets          1) mainsheet
                 2) jibsheet

Sheets are used to control the sails. They are lines which attach to the sail and run to the cockpit.

Luffing: when the sail trembles from insufficient wind or from facing too close into the wind.

Tell-tales: pieces of yarn or ribbon tied to the shrouds and back stay to indicate the direction of the wind.

Roller furling: a type of headsail arrangement which permits the sail to furl in on its own forward wire.

To change direction:
1) tack, come-about
2) jibe

A tack is a change of direction which is accomplished by turning the bow of the boat through the wind. It is also called a come-about.

A jibe is a change of direction made by turning the stern of the boat through the wind. This can be dangerous if done accidentally and not controlled since the boom can swing wildly across the boat.

In irons: facing directly into the wind and unable to sail.

Reefing: reducing the amount of sail surface by lowering the sail and,
1) rolling the sail down and around the boom
or    2) tying off the lower portion of the sail at the boom

Drop the hook: to anchor.

Dinking: commuting from an anchorage in a small boat (a dinghy) which may be towed or carried with the larger boat.

Rafting: when two or more boats tie together at anchor or on a mooring.

Secure: to position or tie down in order to remain stationary.

Fenders: objects used to provide cushioning protection between boat and boat or boat and dock.

Whisker pole: used when running to extend the clew of the headsail out from the boat on the opposite side of the mainsail.

Clew: the lower aft corner of sail.

Boom vang: a block and tackle, rigged between boom and deck, often used to prevent the boom from an accidental swing across the boat.

Gudgeon: a fitting attached to the hull which accepts the rudder's fittings which are called pintles.

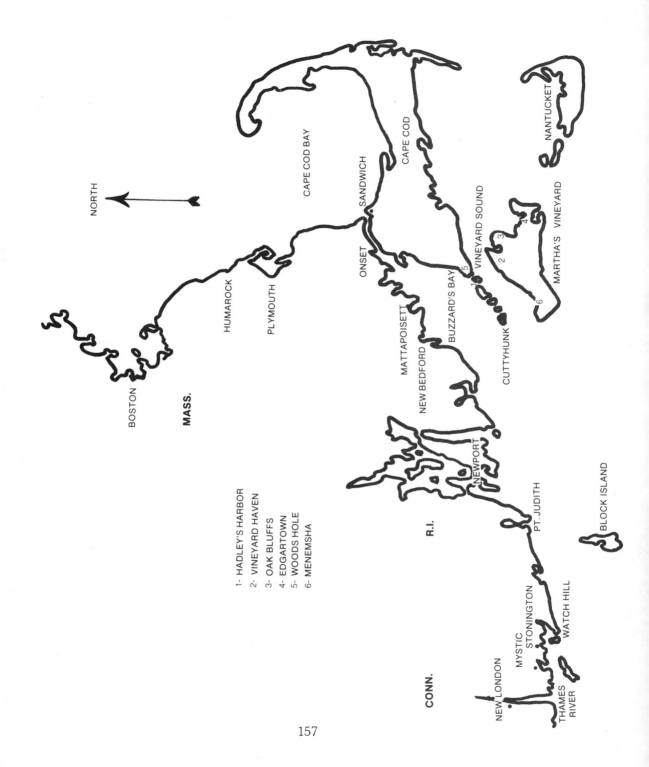

NORTH

CAPE COD BAY

CAPE COD

SANDWICH

NANTUCKET

ONSET

VINEYARD SOUND

MARTHA'S VINEYARD

HUMAROCK

PLYMOUTH

MATTAPOISETT

BUZZARD'S BAY

1
5
2
3
4
6

NEW BEDFORD

CUTTYHUNK

BOSTON

MASS.

NEWPORT

R.I.

BLOCK ISLAND

PT. JUDITH

1- HADLEY'S HARBOR
2- VINEYARD HAVEN
3- OAK BLUFFS
4- EDGARTOWN
5- WOODS HOLE
6- MENEMSHA

MYSTIC
STONINGTON

WATCH HILL

CONN.

NEW LONDON

THAMES
RIVER

157